Oceans and Seas

P9-DJU-604

KINGFISHER
LONDON & NEW YORK

Copyright © Kingfisher 2011
Published in the United States by Kingfisher,
175 Fifth Ave., New York, NY 10010
Kingfisher is an imprint of Macmillan Children's Books, London.
All rights reserved.

Distributed in the U.S. and Canada by Macmillan, 175 Fifth Ave., New York, NY 10010

First published as *Kingfisher Young Knowledge: Oceans and Seas* in 2004
Additional material produced for Kingfisher by Discovery Books Ltd.
First hardback edition published in 2011 by Kingfisher
This paperback edition published in 2013 by Kingfisher

Library of Congress Cataloging-in-Publication data has been applied for.

ISBN: 978-0-7534-6776-3

Kingfisher books are available for special promotions and premiums.
For details contact: Special Markets Department, Macmillan, 175 Fifth Ave., New York, NY 10010.

For more information, please visit www.kingfisherbooks.com

Printed in China
1 3 5 7 9 8 6 4 2

1TR/1212/WKT/UG/128MA

Note to readers: the website addresses listed in this book are correct at the time of going to print.
However, due to the ever-changing nature of the Internet, website addresses and content can
change. Websites can contain links that are unsuitable for children. The publisher cannot be held
responsible for changes in website addresses or content or for information obtained through
a third party. We strongly advise that Internet searches be supervised by an adult.

Acknowledgments
The publisher would like to thank the following for permission to reproduce their material. Every care has been taken to
trace copyright holders. However, if there have been unintentional omissions or failure to trace copyright holders, we
apologize and will, if informed, endeavor to make corrections in any future edition.
b = bottom, *c* = center, *l* = left, *t* = top, *r* = right

Photographs: *cover* Shutterstock Images; 1 Getty; 2–3 Getty; 4–5 Corbis; 6 Getty; 7*tr* National Geographic Image
Collection (NGIC); 7*cl* Nature Picture Library; 7*br* Minden Pictures/Frank Lane Picture Agency; 8–9 Corbis; 9*tl* Alamy; 9*b*
Corbis; 11*b* Corbis; 12–13 Getty; 13*tl* Oxford Scientific Films (OSF); 13*cl* OSF; 13*br* Corbis; 14 Press Association,
London; 15 Corbis; 15*t* Corbis; 16–17 Getty; 16*b* Science Photo Library (SPL); 17*t* OSF; 18–19 Ardea; 19*tl* NGIC;
19*br* Ardea; 20 Getty; 21 Getty; 21*b* Nature Picture Library 22–23 Corbis; 22*bl* Corbis; 23*tl* Getty; 24–25 NGIC; 26*bl*
Nature Picture Library; 27*tl* Nature Picture Library; 27*cr* Nature Picture Library; 27*b* Nature Picture Library; 28–29
Corbis; 28*bl* Getty; 30*b* Getty; 31 Ardea; 31*bl* Ardea; 32*bl* Corbis; 33*t* Minden Pictures/Frank Lane Picture Agency;
33*b* Image Quest 3D; 34–35 Getty; 34*bl* Image Quest 3D; 35*tl* Nature Picture Library; 36–37 Corbis; 36*bl* SPL; 37*tr* SPL;
38 Corbis; 39 Getty; 40*bl* Getty; 40–41 Getty; 41*t* Getty; 48*t* Shutterstock Images/Jan Daly; 48*b* Shutterstock
Images/Alberto Loyo; 49*l* Shutterstock Images/P. Borowka; 49*r* Shutterstock Images/Leksele; 52*l* Shutterstock Images/
R-studio; 52*r* Shutterstock Images/Christian Wilkinson; 53*t* Shutterstock Images/tonobalaguerf; 53*b* Shutterstock
Images/magicinfoto; 56 Corbis

Commissioned photography on pages 42–47 by Andy Crawford
Thank you to models Lewis Manu and Rebecca Roper

Oceans and Seas

Nicola Davies

KINGFISHER
NEW YORK

Contents

Planet ocean

Only one-third of Earth is dry land, so our planet looks blue when it is seen from space. The rest of the planet is ocean, and there is life in every part of it!

an ocean is a large sea

Sunlit surface

The ocean's surface is full of tiny plants and animals called plankton, which are eaten by bigger creatures, such as these jellyfish.

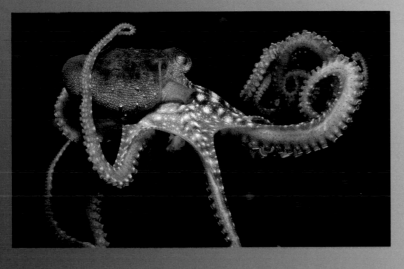

Staying hidden

Many animals, like this octopus, prefer the deeper water of the middle ocean. There, they can hide from predators and be safe from storms.

Deep and dark

The deepest waters are completely dark and cold. Food is hard to find, so animals there have big mouths in order to eat anything!

Salty sea

All seas and oceans are salty, with about half an ounce of salt per pound of water (35 grams per kilogram). That is as salty as one large spoonful of salt in half a bucket of water!

Saltiest sea

The Dead Sea in Asia is so salty that when its water is turned into vapor by the sun, the salt is left behind in hard white lumps.

Salty sources

Volcanic hot spots on land and on the seabed add salt to seawater when they release hot gases and molten rock. Rivers wash salt from the land into the seas and oceans.

Grains of salt

Some of the salt that we put on our food comes from the sea. Sea salt is broken up into small pieces so we can sprinkle it on our food.

Undersea landscape

Hidden under the sea is a world of high mountains, wide plains, and deep valleys—an entire landscape as interesting and varied as the one on dry land!

Flattest and deepest

Almost half of the deep ocean floor is made up of a large, flat area called the abyssal (deep) plain. Even deeper are the ocean trenches, which plunge 32,800 feet (10,000 meters) below the surface.

Mountaintop islands

When volcanoes form on the seabed, they grow into mountains. These can get so tall that they stick out of the sea and make islands.

Black smokers

Deep seawater is usually very cold, but at volcanic spots called black smokers, water three times hotter than boiling gushes through cracks in the seabed.

Tides and waves

Seawater is always moving. It is stirred up by the heat of the sun and the cold of the ice at the North and South poles, pushed by winds, and pulled by the sun and the movement of the moon.

Windy waves

When wind blows over water, it makes waves. Strong winds blowing for a long time make the biggest waves, which can be up to 112 feet (34 meters) high!

Tide out, tide in

The moon pulls water toward it as it goes around Earth, making the seas and oceans bulge away from the coasts. This movement causes tides. Most tides occur twice a day—the sea moves away from the shore (tide out) and back again (tide in).

tide out

tide in

Eating land

In some places, waves wash away beaches and cliffs, changing the shape of the coastline in just a few days.

Weather-making sea

The oceans make weather by warming or cooling the air over them, which creates winds and clouds. Ocean currents carry warmth and cold around the planet.

Hooray for rain!

Clouds from the Indian Ocean bring heavy rains to Asia and Africa. Without the rains, crops would not grow.

Hurricane!

Above warm, tropical seas, air masses can sometimes develop into giant, spinning storms called hurricanes. These storms can move inland and cause enormous damage, destroying entire towns.

El Niño

Every few years, a warm current called El Niño sweeps along the west coast of South America, causing extreme weather across the world—devastating storms, droughts, and even heavy snow!

Living history

Life on Earth began in the sea, billions of years before there was life on land. Some of those early life forms are still alive in the sea today!

First life on Earth?

Stromatolites are mounds of millions of tiny creatures. They look just like stromatolites that lived three billion years ago.

Living fossils

The coelacanth is a fish that was known to us only from million-year-old fossils until, in 1938, a living coelacanth was caught by a fisherman.

Unchanged habits

Each year, horseshoe crabs surface from deep water to lay their eggs on sandy beaches, just as they have for 400 million years!

Fish rule

There are more than 20,000 different kinds of fish in all shapes and sizes, and most of them live in the world's oceans and seas.

Ocean hunters

Big fish, such as this blue shark, are the predators of the sea. Most sharks hunt animals for food and can swim really fast so they can catch their meals.

Fish or seaweed?

The leafy sea dragon
has great camouflage.
It looks so much like
seaweed that it can
hide among the plants
and not be seen by
other fish that might
want to eat it.

Safety in numbers

In a school of fish, there
is a greater chance of
spotting danger (a lot of
eyes) and a smaller chance
of being eaten (many other
fish could be eaten instead)!

Ocean mammals

Sea mammals are shaped for swimming. They have smooth, streamlined bodies that can slip through the water, and they can hold their breath for a long time when they dive.

Sea fliers

Sea lions use their webbed front feet to row them along—fast! It is like underwater flying, and it makes catching fish easy!

Legless dolphins

Dolphins do not have back legs at all! They swim by beating their tails up and down and steer with paddle-shaped feet called flippers.

Sea cows

Dugongs also use their tails and flippers for swimming. These large, heavy animals graze on plants called seagrasses, so their other name is "sea cow."

22 Super sea birds

Sea birds are tough! They fly hundreds or thousands of miles every year to find food at sea. They survive storms and rough seas and still find their way back to land to nest. Phew!

All puffed up

Male frigate birds puff up their bright red chests like balloons to impress female birds and find mates to nest with.

Tiny traveler

The tiny arctic tern travels 15,000 miles (24,000 kilometers) every year, from the Arctic Ocean to the Antarctic Ocean.

Long wings

Huge wingspans of up to 11.5 feet (3.5 meters) carry albatross over the stormiest oceans in search of food.

Diving for dinner

Puffins dive for food, using their wings underwater like paddles. They catch small fish to feed to their chicks on land.

Who eats whom?

Ocean life, just like life on land, depends on plants. Animals that eat plants are called herbivores. The herbivores are eaten by carnivores, or meat eaters. This is called a food chain.

Big mouth, short chain!
The whale shark is the world's biggest fish—up to 50 feet (15 meters) long! Its food chain is very short because it feeds on the smallest animals and plants in the sea—plankton.

killer whale

eats

porpoise

eats

cod

eats

herring

Big mouth, long chain

Killer whales need big
food—they cannot eat tiny
plankton. There are five
links in the food chain
between killer whales and
the smallest plants in the
ocean, called phytoplankton.

eats

zooplankton

eats

phytoplankton

Coral reef

In tropical seas, where the water is warm and clear, corals grow like forests of small pink, yellow, and white trees. They are full of colorful fish and many other kinds of life.

Safe from harm

Little anemone fish can hide from danger among the stinging tentacles of big anemones because anemones never sting their own anemone.

Super slug
The sea slug's bright colors are a warning to predators that it has a sting in its orange skin!

Plantlike corals
Corals look like plants, but really they are animals with soft bodies protected by a hard, stony skeleton. They are related to anemones.

Kelp jungles

All over the world, where the sea is cool and the coastline is rocky, there are underwater jungles of huge seaweeds called kelps.

Jungle eaters

Sea urchins eat kelp, and although they are small, they can munch their way through a forest of seaweed.

. . . and jungle savers

Luckily, many animals eat sea urchins.
Seals, dogfish, lobsters, and sea otters,
such as this one floating in a kelp forest
off the West Coast of the United States,
love to snack on these spiky animals.

Frozen feast

Antarctica is the huge frozen land around the South Pole. It looks like an icy desert, but the ocean around it is full of fish, birds, seals, and whales.

Penguin crowds
Seven kinds of penguins live in the Antarctic, but these Adélies are the most common. There can be five million of them in one nesting area!

Whale schools

Humpback whales, as well as 14 other kinds of whales and dolphins, travel to the Antarctic every summer just to feed.

. . . and here is what they eat . . .

Krill! These shrimplike animals are not big, at just 1.5 inches (4 centimeters) long, but there are a lot of them. A single swarm can cover 45,000 soccer fields and weigh 2 million tons!

Deep oceans

In the deepest parts of the ocean, it is always cold and completely dark. The pressure of water would squash you flat—yet even here, there is life.

Deepest divers

Sperm whales dive 985–9,840 feet (300–3,000 meters) down to feed on giant squid. They can hold their breath for almost an hour!

Silver camouflage

Hatchet fish stay hidden in deep water by having shiny skin that matches the gleam of the water's surface far above.

Shine a light

Some animals make their own light from chemicals in their bodies so that they can find each other in the dark or scare off predators.

Ocean mysteries

Humans have only just begun to explore life in the sea. There is so much we do not know about some of the biggest and most beautiful marine animals.

Giant mystery . . .
The ocean sunfish, or mola, weighs up to 2 tons and eats plankton, but that is almost all we know about this huge fish.

. . . and mysterious giant

Mantas can be 20 feet
(6 meters) across, but like
the ocean sunfish, all we
know about them is that
they swim in the oceans
eating plankton.

Bye-bye baby!

Baby turtles hatch on
sandy beaches and then
disappear out to sea. We
do not know what they do
next, only that they return
many years later to breed
and lay their own eggs.

Studying the sea

The ocean is not our home—we cannot breathe underwater, and we are poor swimmers. However, there are still ways of finding out about the ocean.

Follow that seal!

This fur seal has a radio tag attached to its back. It sends signals that tell scientists where the seal goes and how deep it dives.

Down to the bottom
Tough little submersibles can carry cameras and other equipment to the deepest ocean to find out what goes on there.

Underwater history
Ancient shipwrecks can lie undisturbed on the seabed for thousands of years. Modern scuba (breathing) gear helps divers explore shipwrecks and discover more about human history.

All fished out

For thousands of years, humans have caught fish to eat. In the past, people used simple nets and sailboats. But now that we use motorboats and huge nylon nets, the fish do not stand a chance.

Useless slaughter

Nets catch anything. Every year, millions of dolphins, turtles, sharks, ocean sunfish, and birds die in fishing nets intended to catch something else.

Fishing for trouble

People have become too good at fishing. There are now fewer and fewer fish left to catch. Some fish, such as cod, have almost disappeared!

What a waste!

All over the world, people use oceans and seas as dumps for all types of garbage that kills marine life, but it does not have to be this way.

Stop the spill
If ships carrying oil were made extra strong, oil would not spill so easily when the ships crash.

Safe sewage
Sewage can be made safe enough to spread on farmland, not just dumped into the sea.

Perfect plastic

Plastic trash is ugly and can trap and harm marine animals. This waste can be used again or made so that it breaks down naturally.

Tasty sea slug

You will need:
- Block of marzipan
- Plate
- Food coloring and paintbrush
- Colored candies

A bitter taste

Sea slugs are not eaten by anything in the sea—they taste really horrible! However, here is a sea slug that is tasty to eat.

1

To make the slug's long body, roll the marzipan between your hands into a sausage shape. Then put the shape onto a plate.

2

Many sea slugs have frills. Use your fingers to press down along the bottom edges of the body to make a frill along each side.

3

Dip your paintbrush into some food coloring and paint the frills. The frills can be any color. Paint dots of color down the slug's back.

4

Sea slugs can be very bright. Decorate the slug's body with colored candies. Use two candies as antennae on the slug's head.

Making waves

Wind power

Wind blowing across the sea makes waves. The stronger the wind blows, the bigger the waves are. Find out how in this project.

You will need:
- Large, clear glass bowl
- Water
- Blue food coloring
- Spoon

Fill the bowl half full with water and add a few drops of blue food coloring. Stir the water to mix.

2 Blow across the surface of the water—this is like wind blowing across the sea. Blow hard and you will see large waves.

Paper-plate fish

Shiny scales

Fish come in all sizes, shapes, and colors. Use different colors of shiny paper to make a variety of paper-plate fish.

You will need:
- Pencil
- Paper plate
- Scissors
- Glue and glue brush
- Bottle cap
- 1 sheet of silver paper or foil
- 2 sheets of colored shiny paper
- Black marker

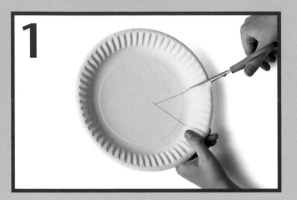

Draw a triangle on the plate and cut it out to make a mouth. Glue the triangle piece onto the body, across from the mouth, to make a tail.

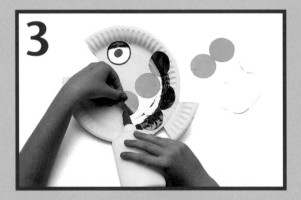

Glue on a silver circle above the mouth and draw a black dot in the center to make the eye. Then stick the other circles onto the body.

Using a pencil, draw around a round bottle cap and make 30 circles on the sheets of shiny paper and foil. Then cut them out.

Sandy starfish

Many arms, but no legs!

Most starfish have five arms, but some have more than 50! They use them to move around and to catch prey.

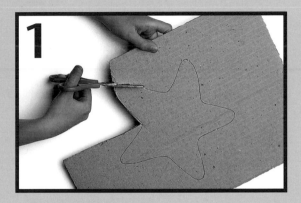

1

Draw a starfish shape on the cardboard and cut it out. Copy the starfish shape from this page.

You will need:
- Thick cardboard
- Pencil
- Scissors
- Glue and glue brush
- Teaspoon
- Orange and pink colored sand

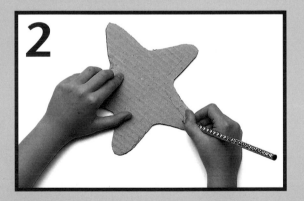

2

Draw a line about half an inch (1cm) from the edge of the starfish, following the starfish shape. Spread glue over the inner starfish shape.

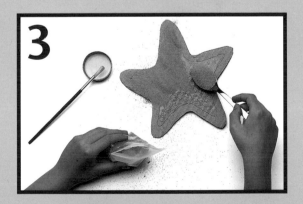

3

Use the spoon to sprinkle on the orange sand. Press down the sand and leave it to dry. Do the same with pink sand on the edge of the starfish.

Jolly jellyfish

Many tentacles

Jellyfish use their tentacles to gather food as they swim. There are more than 200 types of jellyfish, and some have tentacles that are 100 feet (30 meters) long!

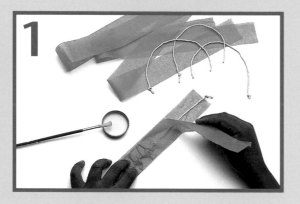

1

Glue each piece of string down the middle of four strips of tissue paper, from top to middle. Fold up the remaining paper to cover the string.

You will need:

- Glue and glue brush
- 4 pieces of string, 8 in. (20cm) long
- Green tissue paper cut into 5 strips, 16 in. (40cm) long
- Scissors
- Colored paper plate
- Tape
- Shiny paper

2

Cut the plate in half. Place each green tissue tentacle onto the back of the plate half and stick each one down with tape.

3

Glue the fifth tissue paper strip along the curve of the plate half. Then cut out circles of shiny paper and decorate the jellyfish body.

Seascape

You will need:
- Glue and glue brush
- Green tissue paper cut into strips
- Blue poster board
- Sand
- Pen or pencil
- Shiny paper
- Scissors

All together
Here, you can create an underwater landscape to show the crafts you have made in this book.

Glue the tissue paper onto the poster board and spread glue over the bottom of the board. Pour sand over the glue and pat it down.

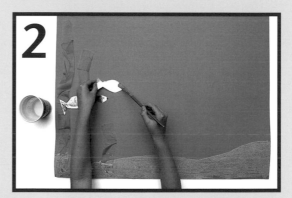

Draw fish on the shiny paper. Cut them out and stick them onto the poster board. You can add any other sea animals you have made.

Use different-colored paper, foil, and sand to make more sea creatures for your seascape.

Glossary

abyssal plain—a large, flat area of land deep on the seabed

billion—1,000 million, written like this: 1,000,000,000

camouflage—a shape, color, or pattern that helps hide an animal

carnivore—a meat-eating animal

coast—the shore, where sea and land meet

current—the movement of seawater within a sea or ocean

fossil—the remains of ancient animals or plants that have gradually turned into rock

herbivore—a plant-eating animal

marine animal—an animal that lives in or on the sea

nylon—tough, synthetic thread

predator—an animal that hunts and eats other animals

pressure—the weight of water in the ocean

radio tag—a device that sends out invisible signals that travel long distances

school—a group of fish swimming
together

sewage—body waste that you
flush down the toilet

streamlined—having a smooth
body shape that moves easily
though the water

submersible—a machine that can
dive underwater

swarm—a large group of small
animals

tentacles—long, flexible parts of
an animal, used for gripping,
feeling, or moving

trenches—long, narrow,
underwater valleys, usually
formed next to islands or
mountains

vapor—a mist or gas given off
when something is heated

volcanic—describes anything to
do with volcanoes

webbed—describes toes that are
joined together by a flap of skin

wingspan—the distance between
a bird's wingtips

zooplankton—a type of plankton
that is an animal, not a plant

The content of this book will be useful to help teach and reinforce various elements of the science and language arts curricula in the elementary grades. It also provides opportunities for crosscurricular lessons in geography, art, design, and math.

Extension activities

Writing
Imagine you are a mighty albatross. You are flying across the great oceans in all kinds of weather, looking for food (pp. 22–23). Write a journal describing your daily experiences for several days.

Literature
Look in the library for books on ocean-related legends: shipwrecks, mermaids, pirates, and more. Which of these stories do you think *could* be true, and which are obviously made-up stories? Look also for true-life adventures and explorations. How would you like to have been a sailor onboard an old-fashioned sailing ship?

Science
The topic of oceans relates to the scientific themes of Earth's features; environments, habitats, and ecosystems; and diversity. Some specific links to science curriculum content include adaptations (pp. 18–23, 32–33); animal defenses (pp. 19, 26–27); behavior (pp. 17–23, 26–35); conservation (pp. 38–41); defense (pp. 27, 32–33); evolution (pp. 16–17); food chains and webs (pp. 24–25, 31); scientific inquiry (pp. 34–37); predator/prey relationships (pp. 6–7, 18–19, 24–27); structure and function (pp. 18–23, 26, 32–35); and weather (pp.14–15).

Crosscurricular links
1) Writing, design, and oral language: Page 32 describes significant challenges to exploring the deepest parts of the ocean. Imagine, design, and describe a vehicle you might use to learn about what is there.

2) Writing, art, and oral language: On a large piece of paper, draw and color a fish of your own design. Write a description, including such things as its habitat, geographic location, predators and prey, defenses, and life history. Give a short oral report about your fish, using your picture as a visual aid.

3) *Geography, math, and writing:* See *www.livescience.com/animals/ Arctic-tern-record-migration-100111.html* for details about the amazing migration of the arctic tern (p. 23). Use this information to plot maps, identify locations, create math problems using data, and write stories.

4) *Geography:* All oceans are connected. The largest areas have names. Seas may be parts of oceans, or they may be enclosed by land. See how many oceans and seas you can find on a world map.

Using the projects

Children can do these projects at home. Here are some ideas for extending them:

Page 42: Use a clear glass baking pan for the wave activity. Wearing safety glasses, blow, tilt the pan in different directions, and otherwise disturb the water. Watch from the sides as well as from above. Float a small cork to see how different waves move it.

Page 43: Use modeling clay to design and make a boat that will float, even when you blow waves at it.

Pages 44–47: Write a short report about each animal and put them together in a booklet. Or make up a story about life in your seascape habitat.

Did you know?

- More than two-thirds of Earth's surface is covered by water.

- The average depth of the ocean is more than 2.5 miles (4 kilometers).

- The world's oceans contain around 20 million tons of gold.

- Ninety percent of all volcanic activity occurs in the oceans.

- The blue whale is the largest animal in the ocean. It's as long as two and a half school buses!

- A tsunami is a huge ocean wave produced by an underwater earthquake.

- The deepest part of any ocean is the Marianas Trench, which reaches a depth of 36,000 feet (11,000 meters) below sea level.

- The world's largest fish is the whale shark. It can grow up to 50 feet (15 meters) long.

- The fastest fish in the sea is the sailfish. It can swim at speeds of up to 68 mph (110km/h).

- Every year, the weight of all the garbage dumped in the sea is three times more than the weight of all the fish caught by fishermen.

- The gray whale migrates 10,000 miles (16,000 kilometers) each year, the farthest distance of any mammal.

- Sea kelp can grow up to 100 feet (30 meters) long.

- The largest ocean in the world is the Pacific. The smallest is the Arctic.

- More people have been in space than have visited the deepest parts of the ocean.

- The oceans contain 99 percent of the living space on the planet.

- The ocean is blue because it reflects blue light rays from the sun.

- There is no marine life in the Dead Sea. It is so salty that plants and fish cannot live there.

Oceans and seas quiz

The answers to these questions can all be found by looking back through the book. See how many you get right. You can check your answers on page 56.

1) How many different kinds of fish are there?
   A—20
   B—200
   C—20,000

2) How large is the wingspan of the albatross?
   A—11.5 feet (3.5 meters)
   B—20 feet (6 meters)
   C—33 feet (10 meters)

3) How far does the arctic tern travel every year?
   A—6,000 miles (10,000 kilometers)
   B—15,000 miles (24,000 kilometers)
   C—22,000 miles (36,000 kilometers)

4) What do whale sharks eat?
   A—plankton
   B—birds
   C—people

5) Where do anemone fish hide from danger?
   A—in a clam shell
   B—under a rock
   C—in the tentacles of anemones

6) Which sea has the saltiest water?
   A—the Red Sea
   B—the Dead Sea
   C—the Caspian Sea

7) What is the other name for a dugong?
   A—sea cow
   B—sea pig
   C—sea elephant

8) How do male frigate birds impress females?
   A—they sing a song
   B—they puff out their chests
   C—they do a dance

9) How many kinds of penguins live in the Antarctic?
   A—1
   B—17
   C—7

10) For how long can sperm whales hold their breath underwater?
    A—60 seconds
    B—1 hour
    C—6 hours

11) What is a group of fish called?
    A—a school
    B—a gang
    C—a squad

12) What is El Niño?
    A—a type of fish
    B—a warm current
    C—a Spanish president

Find out more

Books to read
Explorers: Oceans and Seas by Stephen Savage, Kingfisher, 2010

Far from Shore: Chronicles of an Open Ocean Voyage by Sophie Webb, Houghton Mifflin Books for Children, 2011

Navigators: Oceans and Seas by Margaret Hynes, Kingfisher, 2010

Oceans (True Books) by Peter Benoit, Children's Press, 2011

Viewfinder: Oceans by Barbara Taylor, Silver Dolphin Books, 2011

Weird Ocean by Kathryn Smith, Kingfisher, 2010

Places to visit
Alaska SeaLife Center
www.alaskasealife.org/
Visit the Alaska SeaLife Center and meet many sea creatures, from puffins to sea lions. You can also visit the rescue and rehabilitation center for marine mammals.

The American Museum of Natural History, New York City
www.amnh.org/exhibitions/permanent/ocean/?src=e_h
In the Milstein Hall of Ocean Life, you can learn about marine species and ecosystems, study current issues in ocean conservation, and examine the science of life in water.

Whale watching in Seattle, Washington
www.gonorthwest.com/Washington/seattle/activities/whale_watching.htm
Seattle is a great place to spot gray whales, as well as killer whales. Take a boat trip and see Dall's porpoise, sea lions, and a wide variety of seabirds.

Websites
Fun Ocean Facts
www.sciencekids.co.nz/sciencefacts/earth/oceans.html
This site has a range of interesting facts about the world's oceans as well as information relating to marine life, historical events, and amazing statistics.

All about Oceans and Seas
www.enchantedlearning.com/subjects/ocean/
This site answers many questions about the oceans, including Why is the ocean salty? What causes waves? Why is the ocean blue?

Creatures of the Deep Sea
www.seasky.org/deep-sea/deep-sea-menu.html
At this site you are the controller of a remote, deep-water submarine. Shine its light on the weird and wonderful creatures of the deep and learn about animals such as giant squid, viperfish, and deep sea dragonfish.

Oceans Alive!
www.mos.org/oceans/
Take a closer look at our watery planet. Learn how currents are created, study the water cycle, and find out what scientists get up to at sea.

Oceans and seas
quiz answers

1) C   7) A
2) A   8) B
3) B   9) C
4) A   10) B
5) C   11) A
6) B   12) B